'The Job'
and Beyond

Allen Lewis

Nenge Books, Australia

'The Job' and Beyond
by Allen Lewis

Copyright - text and photographs © Allen Lewis 2021

All rights reserved.

This book or parts thereof may not be reproduced in any form, stored in a mechanical retrieval system or transmitted in any form by any means - electronic, mechanical, photocopy, recording or otherwise - without prior written permission of the publisher.

Design and desktop by Nenge Books
Published by Nenge Books, Australia
ABN 26809396184
nengebooks1@gmail.com
www.nengebooks.com

Nenge Books publishes quality books using cost effective print-on-demand technology to enable independent authors to publish. Enquiries from authors are welcome.

ISBN 978-0-6488889-2-5

Contents

PREFACE	7
EARLY DAYS	9
EARLY WORKING DAYS	15
'THE JOB'	21
COUNTRY VICTORIA	33
THE NORTHERN TERRITORY	39
BACK IN MELBOURNE	67
CHIRNSIDE PARK	70
ARROW INVESTIGATIONS	75
HERVEY BAY	79
GOLD COAST	88

PREFACE

I commenced compiling this book with some trepidation as I had intended to make this effort some years ago when my memory was a little better, in fact, an awful lot better. I had always intended to make notes of my achievements and failures but the years went past, together with my memory, which went past faster. Still, I did not take notes and will have to rely on my present memory which is having a recall now that I have got it started.

As a police officer in both Victoria and Northern Territory I came across some very serious situations and also some very humorous ones, the latter which I will try to concentrate on. In fact, any matters of a delicate nature or of a nature concerning matters where it is likely to involve persons who are still alive or who do not wish to be named, I will change the names accordingly, (referenced with *) although it is very unlikely that it will worry us too much as I recently turned 81 years old.

Allen Lewis
Gold Coast, March 2021

EARLY DAYS

I am now 81 years of age and was born in Armadale, Victoria, Australia in February 1940, which was at the beginning of World War II. My mother lived there with my older brother Glyn and myself. Before we had started school and shortly after my father returned from his army service, we moved to Mitcham, an outer eastern suburb of Melbourne. We lived there for about 12 months before moving again to a 26 acre block at Macclesfield, near Monbulk, in the Dandenong Ranges.

For about twelve months we lived in a large army tent that Dad had borrowed from the army. The local school was about two and a half miles away and we walked both ways as cars in those days were a luxury. I was only five years old at this stage and had attended school for about one year, relying on my older brother to get me to and from. As it turned out, the Fleming family, our neighbours with numerous children, also attended the school. At one time there were eight of them attending, so I was well looked after.

The Fleming family lived about half a mile away where they operated a farm growing fruit trees for sale. There were periods, when it was peak times at the nursery, when the two older boys Don and Maurie did not attend school but stayed at home for the greater part of the time to assist at the nursery. The older siblings built and operated various pieces of machinery which were specifically useful in this type of farming and were either too expensive to buy or needed to be modified to suit the type of business they were used for. Over the next few years I spent more time at Fleming's home than I did at my own and became part of the large family, where I had a lot of meals plus other activities - an extra person was hardly even noticed.

This arrangement suited my mother, as she was pregnant at the time with my sister Gwen who arrived just after I turned seven. Gwen arrived by the side of the road whilst Mervyn Fleming was driving Mum and Dad to the hospital at Ferntree Gully. Dad had spent over half an hour yacking and having a cup of tea before he even asked Nell Fleming if somebody could kindly drive them to hospital. Mervyn was the only one there at the time who had a driver's license so he got the job. Some years later I mentioned it to him and he said he was glad Dad was there, as he had no idea before then what he was required to do. The next day in the paddock he really copped it from his brothers, and the girls kept it up with questions and congratulations all round. Merv, being unmarried at that time, stated that after that experience he would remain single and true to his word he was one of the last of the Flemings to finally marry.

Wherever my father went, he felt it was necessary to have a yarn before one asked a favor. My father, Jimmy Lewis, was a very capable and knowledgeable man and, when looking for work, he would first offer to work for nothing. After a bit more yacking and diversion of conversation he would inevitably get the job.

At one time he was working as a ranger at the nearby Silvan Reservoir which forms part of Melbourne's water supply. Every now and then he would come home with the best and biggest trout I had ever seen, which had apparently been caught in the filters of the main water supply. This had to be removed so it would not contaminate the water but was also part of the job! But of course he was known to partly exist on the BBB philosophy (bull**** baffles brains). That became a great saying and I have used it many times in the ensuing years.

Later, within that period of time, my sister Gwen began to walk to Macclesfield School whilst my brother and I attended Upwey High School, being the only high school in that area at that time. My brother Glyn was very much the academic and was up with anything along those lines whilst I excelled in the sports department and only studied when I needed to, such as the day before exams and other equally unimportant days, which of course my brother considered very important.

Glyn was also a very accomplished long distance runner and won the school cross-country race every year he entered. He also won the mile and half mile events at the interschool sports whilst I won the high jump and long jump events. My brother used to get very annoyed when I was able to win events by just turning up on the day with no training. On his final year at high school it appeared that he was going to have some good opposition in the cross-country race, so he started training and won the event easily - but was annoyed to find out shortly after that his little brother had come in eighth after not having done any training for the event. Later at 16 years of age he was the youngest in the country at that time to complete the marathon event and scored a large write-up on the back page of the Melbourne Sun. He was astounded to read about the interview he had with a sports journalist after the race. He swears he never had that interview!

My father was a very good negotiator and, through the local Member for Parliament, was able to secure a school bus which went to Upwey High School exclusively - acommodating my family, a few others and the large family of Flemings, although some of them had left school by that time. The older boys Len, Ken, and Merv went to work on the family farm whilst Connie and Myra were doing domestic duties. Marj went to work in Melbourne which left Don, Maurie, Ray, Beryl and Thelma to attend school though Don and Maurie were absent for a good part of the year doing nursery duties. These boys taught me the game of cricket and at the age of 16 I enjoyed it enough and was good enough to join the Monbulk Cricket team. The team contained five Fleming brothers and they were all so talented that it was difficult for me to get in to bat because the Fleming boys took over the batting crease and hardly ever got given out. But at my age to win a number of cricket flags was quite remarkable.

At the age of 14 I played AFL football for Silvan but the majority of my friends played for Monbulk, so the following football season I swapped over and played for Monbulk. As I was already at my maximum height of six feet two. Playing in the ruck position I was fair game for the older players to knock me around but it did not take long to learn how to defend myself and get plenty of ball at the same time. Earlier in the text I wrote about my prowess at school and being the high jump champion. This augured well for me for the majority of my football rucking duties, but I still carry the legacy of one such encounter to this day. Fortunately it has never worried me to any great extent until very recent times when I

'The Job' and Beyond

over-balanced in this very room, fell against the corner of my desk and fell right on the rib that I had injured many years previously.

I had been fortunate to be selected in a combined Mountain District team to play against Dandenong, who were a very high ranked team in the Victorian Football Association. I was immediately targeted by their number one ruck man who 'ran me over' at the start of the game. Monbulk Football Club at that time was zoned in the area of Hawthorn and they often sent talent scouts to various games when they had had a tip off about a particular player. On this day they attended the match against South Belgrave as they'd had a tip off about the prowess of Ray Fleming, the youngest of the Fleming boys, who had shown a lot of promise. But on this day I played very well and received the Hawthorn trophy for a best on ground performance plus an invitation to attend training at Hawthorn at the commencement of the following football season.

I had at that time commenced employment in an office in Melbourne and met Roy Baldwin, who was a former Hawthorn player of great prowess, and he gave me an extra boost by arranging a training run with the senior team and the great Peter Hudson. I continued training with the Under 19 squad and, after playing in a couple of games with the squad, could not feel any positive vibes. So I bade farewell to the Hawks and went back to Monbulk and fronted my mates. And need I say more about them when I mentioned Peter Hudson.

I continued playing with the U17 team on Saturday mornings and then followed up with the senior team in the afternoon. I was runner-up for the District U17 best and fairest behind a South Belgrave player Bob (Nails) Carmichael. Bob continued on playing football for another season, then swapped sports and became an international tennis player. I would like to point out that I was a very distant second behind Bob Carmichael.

EARLY WORKING DAYS

I decided I had better earn my keep so, with my mother's help I applied for an advertised position as Junior Draftsman in an office at the Melbourne and Metropolitan Board of Works, now known as Melbourne Water. I waited about three weeks and finally received a reply asking me to present myself for an interview on a date which had already past! Over the next week or ten days I attempted to find another position of a similar type but before I could do so, I received a letter in the mail stating that I had been appointed to the originally advertised position and to present myself to start about a week later. How easy is this employment business? But I genuinely felt sorry for whoever it was who missed out. I never did find out whose chair I was sitting on.

Being the junior of the office required me to do tasks of a mundane nature, such as getting the boss his morning cup of tea. Yes, I was the errand boy and the job required me to run around the whole building doing simple things such as picking up a file and delivering it to some other person who needed it, so consequently I didn't learn very much. This all changed for the better when I got to know Roy Baldwin, the former Hawthorn footballer. I had started work at the Board of Works, to do a Civil Engineering Degree and become a surveyor, so I started doing one afternoon at school and two evenings at night school. After taking on this 27 subject course, and after passing five subjects I learnt that the course had been increased by five subjects. It is called Lewis Luck and I decided very quickly and easily to make further enquiries regarding employment.

Working at the Bureau of Works

I saw an advertisement in the newspaper to join the Police Force, and immediately made up my mind what I wanted to do. The advert in the newspaper was a breath of fresh air and certainly something to look forward to so I applied to join the force. The drafting job was interesting so I stayed put for a while and easily adapted to drawing various types of water mains and fittings. I was not as enthralled when it came to pay day, and I duly received seven pounds fifty per fortnight, whilst I noted that the Police Force had a starting salary of twenty-six pounds per fortnight

About two months later I received notification that if I was still interested, the next intake of police was taking place on the 19th December 1959. I decided to take it on. It was an almost four months course and what I would describe as intense. The big day was graduation day and

'The Job' and Beyond

I was fearful that if I came last in the class they would give me the DCM (Don't Come Monday). To make matters worse, it turned out that graduation day was on April 1st, April Fools Day. However it turned out all ok as I didn't come last, just second last, and then next day after a bit more paperwork, the fitting of uniforms, issue of equipment, it was out there in the action.

I was allocated a room on the first floor and our Instructor showed us the important facilities such as the dining room and the Notice Board, which stated in large capital letters 'NO ENTRY AFTER 11PM' and text written, also in large letters, which read 'THIS TIME MEANS WHAT IT SAYS, NO EXCEPTIONS'. The rooms were basic but small and neat and a demonstration was given by our instructor where to find dust when cleaning the room. He then climbed on to the bed, then onto the front bedrail, reached up to the picture rail and ran his finger along it. One could almost take bets on the fact that he put the dust in the room purely for the demo. However, I daren't suggest that at the time as I would probably be a receiver of the DCM myself.

As we walked into the building I noticed that to get into my room I had to go down some stairs, past a storeroom with some wooden furniture stacked outside the door, then up another stairway, and along to my room at the other end of the building. This seemed an imposition at the time as I and the other new recruits wondered why it was so difficult to get to our rooms. The very same night we heard some angry voices and one of them was that of our instructor. He had nobbled one of the new guys as he was entering the building at 11.10pm, and was getting the rounds of the table for getting in late when he knew what the curfew was.

There was plenty of yelling and bad language, then all went quiet.

The following night I heard some noises that indicated to me that our new recruit had just arrived home. Shortly afterwards there was plenty of shouting, but this time from one person only. About 30 seconds later I heard footsteps running along the front passage towards the stairway, down the stairway towards the storeroom. After a lot more shouting and bad language, we were all ordered out of bed and made to line up outside the rec room. Apparently the same fellow from the night before had restacked the furniture outside the storeroom, removed the light globe from its socket, and made a noise - of course the second noise he heard was the sergeant falling over the furniture in the dark. Nobody, including the sergeant, ever found out the truth of who did the furniture stacking and who removed the light globe from its socket. Even the expert fingerprint man could not find anything. Boys will be boys.

During my time in the Police Academy, and being the tallest in the squad, I became the right marker on the parade ground and, towards the end of the stay, we practised on the parade ground for our graduation ceremony.

During one of these practice sessions the office-in-charge leaned over and said to me, "Are you playing footy for Monbulk next season? If your answer is in the negative, there is a vacancy in the ruck at South Belgrave".

He then stood up straight and continued with the practice. Geoff Beasley was his name and he was a crack shot with a pistol. One afternoon, when he was in charge at Boronia, a fellow came along to the police station and sprayed an array of bullets, smashing the door and windows. This man was well known to the police officer after the service of a warrant the day before the incident and was told to discard the rifle and put his hands up. He fired more shots at the police station so Beasley fired at him and the problem was solved. As a result of this occurrence where a firearm was discharged, and with the usual criticism from the police department and the press, he retired on medical grounds about 12 months later, never believing at the time of the incident that it would have affected him so severely.

During the latter part of my police training at St Kilda Road Depot I went out one evening to one of my regular haunts, Ziggy's Dance Hall in Auburn, to their regular Tuesday night dance. I was attracted to a young lady during the interval of the barn dance and invited her to have drinks with me during the longer interval. From there on we had every dance until the end of the evening and I offered to drive her home to Surrey Hills, together with her sister who was accompanying her. She became my constant companion. About two years later we got engaged and have been together ever since. Her name is Joy and she forms part of this publication. Her name is as good as her nature and she has given me the encouragement to put this story together.

Victorian Police Academy Graduation 1960; Allen in uniform

'THE JOB'

My first posting for duty was 'on the beat' around the city of Melbourne and doing the dreaded beat around Parliament House on night shift. The beat consisted of patrolling around the building, which was corner to corner and taking twenty minutes to complete the section, not knowing when the Inspector would arrive, which could be anytime during the section or sometimes not at all.

Following on from there I was posted to Fitzroy, where accommodation was provided, so I managed to secure a room on my own. All my patrols were done with a superior officer and I gained a lot of experience in a very short time. But I soon found out there were people where I worked with reputations which left me a bit cold.

There was a sergeant who was temporarily put in charge of Fitzroy whilst his colleague was on leave. He was unusual from the point of view that he never held a driver's license. He was generally quite well liked in police circles and also with most of the public he dealt with. The police station was on a piece of land adjacent to Fitzroy Court House. As I lived at the police station I also parked my car there together with other residents. I was out in the patrol car one morning and returned to find my car resting on the fence on the other side of the road from where I had parked it. The front of the car was smashed up. I found out who the culprit was and duly confronted him. I was told in no uncertain terms I could get the car fixed myself and, if I wanted to pursue the matter I would also get six months night shift. I had got to know the Clerk of Courts rather well and I went and had a chat with him. He made out a summons (which was not signed or stamped) but when I served it on the sergeant he was unaware it was not legal. All I got from him was a very big sigh and he asked how much he owed me. When I said $380 he said it was only worth half that amount, unlocked the bottom drawer of his desk and paid the amount requested. I still got the two weeks night shift though!

Shortly after that I managed to get a transfer to the Kew police station, which was not quite as intense as Fitzroy. Just before I left Fitzroy I spent my last week on the night shift doing foot patrols around Fitzroy and Collingwood. I was very fortunate to have as my companion Sergeant Dennis Barrett, who taught me quite a lot. He is mentioned in greater detail later in the text, where he was directly involved in the Lindy Chamberlain murder trial in the Northern Territory.

At Kew, one of the regular duties was traffic control morning and afternoon at the five-way Kew Junction. All staff at the police station were required to participate and control the junction traffic, whilst having the traffic light changed manually from the switchbox on the corner of the intersection by a second member. This was a welcome change of duties and we got to control the traffic for people we knew and make the cycle a little longer if we saw them coming in the distance. It made the job more light-hearted, as one was able to help out people and allowed then to get to their employment a few minutes earlier. Consequently, when the traffic was heaviest on special days or on Christmas holiday break-ups, the man controlling in the centre of the junction often stood there with many presents surrounding him. These were later shared with other traffic controllers. However, normal police duties were undertaken once the traffic cleared.

On one afternoon a lady came into the police station in a distraught state and said that her two year old boy had been out in the garden and had eaten some leaves from a rhus tree, which was known to be poisonous and could be fatal if not treated within a short time. Together with one of the policewomen, we got the car out and rushed him to St George's Hospital, which was only a few hundred metres away. They refused to deal with the matter, as they said they had nobody there who could treat him, and we were advised to take him to St Vincent's Hospital, which was about seven kilometers away on the fringe of Melbourne city. The policewoman was an extremely good driver so she drove whilst I contacted headquarters who arranged for an ambulance to meet us half way. However we were travelling so fast and so well we arrived at the hospital just after the ambulance left so delivered the boy to the hospital ourselves. The mother was most grateful and thanked us for our efforts, but unfortunately the little boy died as he was being taken into the hospital and was unable to be revived. Consequently, for many years after that I found it difficult to deal with any matters where small children were involved.

The Kew CIB was very much involved in some large criminal cases and, after helping them out by sitting in on a number of interviews, I also was involved in giving evidence in the court cases that went with them.

I developed a keen interest in the courts and their workings, which augured well in later years when I had my own investigation business and had to attend court on many occasions.

As a result of getting involved with other staff at Kew we formed a police basketball team and competed in the second division of the Business Houses Competition. This was a constant commitment and those who were available competed every Tuesday night. Sometimes it was difficult to get enough players to put a team on the court due to us all doing shift work at different times. I was also very much involved in the Victoria Police Basketball team which traveled to various venues around the State playing against the local teams. It was quite a serious exercise and, as far as any injuries were concerned, it was classified as 'on duty'.

At that time barrister and solicitor, Maurice Goldberg, who was very highly regarded in his profession, was living in Kew. He often had cases at the Kew court, but he mostly had cases involved in Supreme Court matters which were more attune to his ability. As he lived in the nearby area, and, being a single man, he often dropped in for a yarn with the local police. As a consequence, I knew him quite well.

One particular day I had a case in the local court and the defendant had been involved in a minor matter which he would normally have pleaded guilty to but, on the advice of Mr. Goldberg, his defense counsel, he pleaded not guilty. After a plea from his counsel he was found not guilty and discharged on a technicality. I was disappointed at the outcome as I believed he was guilty. I went back to the police station and tried to work out what I had done wrong, particularly after my sergeant said I was correct in my presentation and evidence. A few minutes later Mr. Goldberg appeared and apologized for the defendant being found not guilty but congratulating me on my evidence, saying, "Don't worry, I will fine him". Maurice was true to his word and charged the culprit what I considered an exorbitant amount for his services.

He also said to organize a party and a tennis competition. He said it was an 'order' because if nobody played tennis on his court which was next to his home in Studley Park Road, he would have to build a block of units on it. We duly complied with his request and, one morning, six of us from the police station had a morning of tennis, doing our best to empty his refrigerator of quite a few stubbies of beer which had been cooling off for far too long. I was very glad that he did not have any matters before the courts that afternoon as he would have slept right through them.

By this stage, Joy and I had made plans to be married on April 27, 1963 at St. Francis Xavier Church on Whitehorse Road, Box Hill, with the Reception at Wattle Park chalet in Riversdale Road. We had commenced building our new house in Lightwood Drive, Ferntree Gully. I had just organized a transfer to Burwood Police Station, as it was very direct to travel to and from our home straight along Burwood Highway, taking about 15 minutes. After the guys at the police station found out the date of the wedding and the time, I was expecting some prank by them just before the ceremony occurred. Just as the ceremony was about to start I heard police sirens in the distance and waited for the next move, which fortunately never came. False alarm!

After the wedding came the honeymoon and we drove north and had ten days on Heron Island in Queensland. After returning home we moved into temporary accommodation in Box Hill while our house was being completed, and Joy returned to her occupation as a primary school teacher at St John's Catholic Primary School in Ferntree gully teaching prep. and first graders. Joy continued teaching until the birth of our son Darryl, who turned into a delightful child and in some ways a 'chip off the old block'. My police duties at this time were still at Burwood.

It may be prudent at this stage to write about the prowess of my father-in-law, Vic Hetherington, who was also a policeman and stationed at Blackburn, where he remained for a lengthy period of time before taking over duties in charge of Marysville, Victoria. I had a great deal of respect for Vic, whose capabilities were boundless and, even though he decided on a career in the Police Force, could have taken on any occupation and done it successfully and well.

Burwood Police Station was one of the more interesting places I worked from and the personnel on any given shift were fascinating. The senior sergeant in charge was Sergeant Eric Senior and, yes that was his name. He said that as a junior he was called Constable Senior, which was correct, and as a senior constable he was addressed as Senior Senior, also correct! Second in charge was Senior Constable Alex McGregor, then came First Constables James Cusack, Garth Higgins and Bob Bennett, and Constables Ron Taylor, Roy Beasley, Geoff Beasley, Wayne Pauley and myself. Each one had talents purely of their own and if you wanted to do something, go somewhere or fix something, it was just a matter of asking around.

Ask Alex McGregor about musical instruments and in particular reeds for oboes and, in particular, his oboe - he knew all about it as he played in the Victorian

Symphony Orchestra. Garth Higgins was a motor mechanic extraordinaire and owned and loved two Citroen Goddess cars, one of which he loaned to us in later years when we were on leave from Darwin. Bob Bennett was an ex North Melbourne Football player and a champion police boxer.

Ron Taylor was a man who is practically indescribable. He was about 6'4", very good looking and the greatest overall athlete I have ever known. He competed as Australian Heavyweight boxer at the Rome Olympic Games. He qualified also to compete in the double sculls but chose not to compete in both disciplines as, in his words, he would not be able to give his all in both sports. He said that, although he gave his all, the powers that be didn't and he lost in the first round of the boxing. He confessed that it wasn't a bad thing as he had never been to Rome and was able to do some sight-seeing. He was also a great AFL player and he played in the vicinity of 50 games for St Kilda and South Melbourne, the latter club now known as the Sydney Swans. He was also the Victorian Police boxing champion and very well respected amongst the members, being very well spoken and groomed. I had the pleasure of working with him on many occasions.

One Sunday morning a call came through to the Burwood Police Station from the nearby Catholic Church. Father Jenkins stated that his Poor Box had been broken into overnight and monies stolen. Ron answered the call and stated we would be there in a few minutes as it was only a few hundred metres away. I accompanied him and we met the priest just outside the front door of the church. He thanked us for arriving so promptly and he entered through the foyer with Ron and me just behind him. He went through the double doors and into the church. When facing the altar he genuflected on one knee and blessed himself. Ron, who was immediately behind him, could not stop in time and went straight over the priest and landed on the carpet in front of him. It was all too much for me, so I exited and burst into laughter and found myself laughing on and off for the rest of the day. So did Ron, but he was a bit embarrassed although he would not admit it. There were numerous times when laughter was the best medicine, some of which will appear later in the book.

Whilst working the night shift Divisional Van and patrolling in the Auburn area, my partner and I received a call on the police radio that a man had been sighted attempting to enter a warehouse, but it appeared he had got stuck in the window and couldn't move. We attended the scene and found a short dark man stuck up to about his waistline in a factory window. It then appeared that the older style sliding window had slipped down and he was stuck and could not move. It appeared that he initially used a ladder which had fallen over when the window slid down on him.

When inquiring of his reasons for being there in the first place, he said that he owned the business and was there trying to fix the window. When inquiring as to what he manufactured there he replied, "concrete blocks". A further inspection of the place showed that he was indeed caught with a rope around his ankle, which was attached to a concrete block with a pulley attached, but the pulley had jammed, letting the window down and jamming him in the frame. He did in fact own the factory and did make various types of concrete shapes.

However later we were told that the man who called police in the first place was found to have decorative concrete blocks in his nearby back yard and the owner was trying to fix a lock on the window to stop him getting in.

The police station at Burwood was situated in an area called a quiet zone and was basically crime free with low traffic, which enabled the personnel to be switched around at a moment's notice. Whilst this suited some officers such as me, it didn't suit others so they stayed at the base whilst others looked after the outside duties, which meant anything from football matches to concerts or testing new equipment. Sergeant Senior was well aware that I was quite happy to do this work so he quite often rang me at home and I went straight to the venue wherever it might be. One of my favourites was duty at the football, mostly at the MCG and these varied from the home-and-away games to the almost certain duties at the finals. I was stationed at Burwood for five years and was fortunate to attend five AFL Grand Finals.

Duties also involved looking after the big names at the concerts at what was then known as West Melbourne Stadium. I looked after the Beatles, both at the stadium and their hotel. At the Stadium I also looked after Johnny O'Keefe, Bill Haley and the Comets, Little Richard, The Platters and Charlie Pride and, when the Rolling Stones did their first Melbourne Concert at St Kilda Town Hall, I was asked to look after the backstage area. And, yes, Mick Jagger does wear lipstick as I saw him put it on. At the same time Roy Orbison was the support act and he approached me for a chat. He said that he was a little more relaxed if he took his mind off the concert for a few moments.

With others, I was also asked if I would go to Melbourne University and, over a three day period, consume alcoholic drinks, small meals, more drinks, more eats, all interspersed with readings taken from a machine called a breath analyzer. It was not very often that my boss arranged for me to be driven to a venue where all I was going to do that day was have a few drinks over a period of time and then be driven home again when it suited me.

When Sergeant Senior came around looking for volunteers to attend the Police Advanced Driving School I jumped on board straight away. The driving school was run by Senior Constable Keith Halliwell, who was a fanatic behind the steering wheel of a car. He was a great driver and a member of the Police Motor Sports Club which won the Bathurst 500 mile race, driving one of the PMSC Studebaker Larks capable of being driven at 150-170 mph. We had 12 participants for this section of the driving school and we did speed tests, braking tests, rough country roads, high speeds on winding roads, the skid pan as it was then called, and we participated in travelling 100mph on the Geelong to Melbourne motorway.

What they called the skid pan was a large section of concrete slab with water running across it, another with oil running across it and a third where both water and oil crossed it together. This was a five week course and at the end we had to be competent to drive across it without skidding off the road and the same while braking or steering. However, it was a great thrill to learn I had come first in the driving course. Keith Halliwell was a great instructor and was the only person who could drive fast into the slippery slide and spin the car at least 15 times. When I tell that story people often ask "Was he allowed to do that?" and my usual answer to that one is simply, "Boys will be boys!". His fellow instructors could not match him.

The year came when it became compulsory for all drivers to wear a seat belt when driving on all types of roads. The powers that be were having difficulties getting people to comply, so they introduced a TV advert that showed what could happen if you were involved in a head-on collision. The dummies in the advert went straight ahead, bounced off the windscreen then flew backwards and it was announced that they certainly would have died.

Next morning, around 2am, we received a radio call asking my partner and me to attend the scene of an accident in Whitehorse Road, Toorak, where it appeared on brief inspection that an expensive Alfa Romeo had struck a power pole. There were two occupants in the front seats of the car who appeared to be deceased. An ambulance was immediately called, arrived within a few minutes and our belief that the occupants of the car had died at the scene were confirmed. It was hard to believe that we had just witnessed live a replica of the TV advert which had been launched only hours earlier.

Senior Constable Bob Bennet lived about 1km from the Burwood Police Station. He was an interesting fellow who was a very good footballer and played many games for North Melbourne. He was very fit and worked out at the gym every day. He had a lot of difficulties with a man who lived a few houses away from him. This man was aware of Bob's occupation and taunted him constantly. One particular night he taunted him again whilst Bob's wife was in the street. He then ran inside and came out carrying a large knife. In the meantime, Bob had phoned the police station and Constable Ron Taylor was on his way, while the offender had returned inside to get a second knife which he waved at the police. Ron Taylor crouched in his best boxing stance and delivered two of his best left hand punches at the offender's face. With the first one he dropped the offender to his knees and the second hit Bob flush on the chin and dropped him to his knees as well. Eventually they managed to subdue the neighbor and take him to the cells at Camberwell, a 24 hour station.

A few weeks later, whilst again doing night patrol duties, we received a message from police radio D24 to keep a lookout for three boys who had failed to return to the local boys' home. About an hour on we received a call that three boys were interfering with parked cars and letting down the tyres. As it turned out, they were the three boys we were looking for so we managed to find a pump for inflating car tyres and put them to work. However, the next morning we were summoned to our inspector's office, given a scolding for the tyre pumping incident and were told this was regarded as summary justice which was not listed in the rule book. The boys lived temporarily at the boys' home in Elgar Road where there were six homes in a row, three for boys and three for girls. One of the nurses at the girls' home was well known to us due to our dealings with wayward children but we will note more about her later on. Her name was Maureen.

COUNTRY VICTORIA

After Burwood I decided to get some country town experience so I transferred to Heyfield, which was approximately half way between Traralgon and Maffra in the area known as South Gippsland. Shortly before transferring to Heyfield I had applied for a transfer to Port Moresby where I would have been classified as a sub-inspector. I was informed that the housing situation at Port Moresby was not good so we shelved that idea and settled in at Heyfield.

As well as playing in the local football team which competed in the Latrobe Valley Football League, playing in the Sale District Basketball Competition and coaching the ladies Basketball team, I managed to fit in some police work. The Sergeant in charge of the police station, Mick Powney, said that it was more public relations and a matter of presence that was mainly required. We made a pact that should anything of a more serious nature occur we would both attend, no matter what time of the day or night.

One such event occurred not long after I arrived. It involved a couple who lived adjacent to the No.1 mill and, according to Sgt. Powney, every pay day at the mill, and any other day for that matter, it was necessary to quieten them down otherwise it could cause the whole area to get involved. The wife was the noisiest, so upon our arrival we immediately resolved to place her in the car and transported her back to the station where we placed her in the cell. We then drove back to her home and found her partner walking up and down the street yelling obscenities at anyone he saw - and he didn't make any exceptions for people driving police cars. We put him in the car and took him back to the station, and deposited him in the cell with his wife. The cell was so small there was not enough room to fight, so in a few moments, all was quiet. Problem solved.

Heyfield was a typical country town with two hotels. The Commercial and the Railway Hotels were privately owned by the one company, which also owned the five sawmills still running. The week before I arrived Sgt. Powney spread the word that I was moving in the following weekend and was bringing the breathalyzer with me. That particular weekend it was noted that there were very few cars about and the hotels had very few customers. On the Monday following, the local taxi driver called at the station to thank us for the best weekend he had had for a long time.

The mill hands and the truckies were hard workers and hard drinkers. The latter believed that they owned the place, and competed with each other to see who could bring the biggest and heaviest load of timber down the mountain in the one day, one week and so on. One milling season, which was mostly summertime, I went for a trip up into the mountains to understand how they loaded the log trucks, and how they drove them. I rode this day with a man named Billy Brown (sounds more like an alibi than a name). Once he had loaded the truck he then filled with water the large tank set behind the cabin of the truck. It was used to pump water on to the brakes to cool them so they could get down the mountain safely, where as if the opposite occurred and the brake discs got red hot, we would never have a hope of stopping and the results of that would be a disaster. As we were now travelling down the mountain, I asked Bill what size load we were carrying. His reply was that he would rather discuss that when we got to the bottom, which indicated to me he was overloaded. Shortly afterwards he said we were carrying 43 cubic tons, which I found out later was the largest load they had transported from that area.

Being a newbie in town they believed that I would grant them favors if they were nice to me. That was a bit of a 'yes and no' situation and depended on their individual attitude towards road safety. One time when I visited the hotel off duty, I was surprised when it appeared that every guy who was on the premises wished to buy me a beer. Later on the following day I got a call from the hotel Manager who stated that he was having some difficulties with two men who refused to leave the premises and he feared a fight with the truckers. I was at the police station, so it was only a minute to arrive at the hotel. The Manager again asked the two men to leave the premises and they again refused. I then asked them the same and, when they again refused, I said that they would be removed forcibly if they would not do as I asked.

One of the men said, "You and what army?".

Immediately all of the twelve men in the bar stood up and one man said, "That's us".

The offenders immediately left the premises; I then knew I had been accepted as a local.

The area covered by the Heyfield police station was the largest in the State and it covered many miles of roadwork just to finalize a few files. In fact it was necessary to take a whole day to cover the whole area. When I arrived at Heyfield I used my own car for police work and charged mileage, which was claimed back from the government once a month.

After using my own car for about two months we were supplied with a brand new police car, and a few days after its arrival the inspector came across from Sale Police headquarters to 'do the books'. Later that morning I was driving along the main street, feeling very conspicuous in the brand new police car, when a car suddenly emerged from the parking area and almost collided with the police car. I immediately indicated for the car to pull over into a parking space and I booked the lady driver for failing to give way. Later that morning I returned to the station and I was asked to meet the inspector. He congratulated me on my manners when I booked the lady driver that morning. It was the inspector's wife, who had come with her husband for a day out.

Then there was Jack, who would often just drop in to the police station for a chat. He mostly came on Monday afternoons and he would report anything that had come to his attention over the weekend. He also stressed that anything he heard at the police station would be strictly for his ears and he would tell nobody about anything he had heard. This information was, of course, very useful to us if we wanted something known around town; we just told Jack the matter was secret and we could guarantee it would be known almost the same day, and certainly by the next. Such as when I arrived in town everybody knew I was bringing the breathalyzer with me, or they were led to believe that it was true. During the period that I was stationed there I was required to test people for their driving licenses.

One morning, whilst Vic and I were both on duty, one of the truck drivers brought his daughter in to the station to be tested for her licence. I was assured by her father that she was a competent driver. I volunteered to take her out for the test with her father sitting in the rear seat. I do believe that her father thought he could influence my decision with him sitting in the rear seat. In fact, after driving only about half my usual route I asked her to return to the police station as she was nowhere near the standard I expected, even for driving on country roads with very little traffic. Her father was most upset when I failed her, and he was quickly out of the car and stated that he would discuss the matter with my sergeant. It was to no avail as he was told that I was doing the test and she needed to come back some other time when she had had more practice. She came back with her father after two weeks had gone by and he asked if Sgt. Powney could take her for the test drive. The wish was granted but she once again failed.

I was only at Heyfield for about eight months and it was a very enjoyable experience, but I decided to take up a position in Darwin in the Northern Territory Police Force.

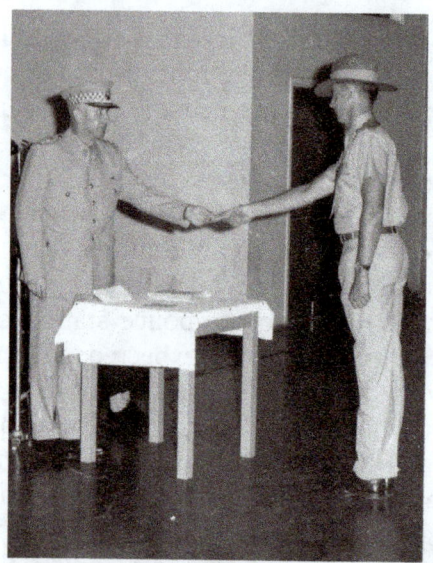

NT Police Graduation 1968

Fishing in South Alligator River.

THE NORTHERN TERRITORY

In June 1968 I commenced the long trip by car which, without the need to hurry, took about 3 days. I had managed to contact another ex-Queensland Police Officer who was also travelling to Darwin to do the same thing, so we teamed up and travelled together which was a good idea from a safety point of view. We duly arrived in the early afternoon of the third day, made the contact at Police Headquarters and were shown to a building in Mitchell Street next to the Koala hotel/motel. This was to be our home for the next few months, after which our families would arrive. It was an ideal set up for single men, as it provided some catering at weekends, looked after us through the week and was within walking distance to the Police Training Depot which was an ideal fitness venue while waiting for my family to arrive.

Joy arrived at the end of that time with our little fellow Darryl in tow and we settled into a unit which was adjacent to the CBD and next to the squash courts to await the arrival of our second child. This was temporary accommodation only until a house became available. Even though it was the middle of the dry season, the weather was still hot, but we soon found it was the ideal climate for all ages and the 'dry' season, as it was known, was magnificent. The climate, particularly the dry season, was very easy to get used to as it was the same for at least six months of the year, and unsettled for the other six months with rain, humidity, and storms. Our daughter, Janine, was born in October at Darwin Hospital.

Not long after Joy arrived in town, we were standing at the rear of the units chatting with our new neighbors when a car entered the carpark at high speed, followed closely by another car in which appeared to be two plain clothes policemen. He gave us the impression that he was trying to get away from the police, so I dived and grabbed him round the legs and brought him to the ground. The following policemen quickly got the handcuffs on him and then came and thanked me for my actions and suggested that I should join the Police Force - we all had a good laugh about it when I told them who I was. Another man had apparently seen the incident and came over and offered himself as a witness. I later learned that he was the editor of the local newspaper. This was my introduction to the Northern Territory Police and I had at that stage not even commenced official duties.

By this time the Aussie Rules Football and Basketball Competitions were just starting and, as I had already become a member of the Waratah Sports Club, I did not take long to get myself signed up for both sports. It was nearing the end of the dry season and, although it was becoming a little humid, it was a constant 28 degrees during the day and about 18 degrees at night, ideal for active sports. The sports training was finished by about 6pm and, one night as I headed home, a young aboriginal man about 24 years of age who lived on my home route, requested a ride to his home, to which I readily agreed. Bob (his aboriginal name was not pronounceable) lived on the Reserve on Bagot Road in one of the transition homes which were set aside for indigenous families to try the mode of living that we had adopted. In Bob's case he had a wife and three children, a steady job at the RAAF base as a gardener, was very well spoken, did not drink or smoke. His general demeanor was exemplary.

As even he had difficulty pronouncing his own surname, he decided to adopt my name of Lewis because, he explained, I was like a brother the way I treated him; so he became Bobby Lewis. Bob was a very good footballer, and easily filled a spot in the senior team. One evening I was driving Bob home from football training when he requested I stop at the take away shop as he had to take home some food for dinner. Sometime later he came out with an extremely large parcel which I questioned him about as I knew the size of his family. It appears because he was the only one with a steady job he was feeding half the village. I never saw him much after that but I believe that not long after that incident he packed up and went back to the Mission on Elco Island. He had succumbed to the system. A very sad affair as far as I was concerned.

Whilst on the subject of people with dark skin, I was on patrol one night when there was a disturbance at Bagot reserve and I received a message to meet the complainant at the front gate. When I arrived there I stopped at the front gate as requested but could not see anybody, so I called out, and the next thing I saw was a set of white teeth next to the car window and about 30cm from my face. Needless to say I got quite a fright, particularly when the teeth spoke to me. I related this little story to my friend Bob, and all he could do was laugh.

After a period, I was posted to the radio room to look after the outback daily radio schedules and to be on hand in case something urgent happened, although that was reasonably rare. Something like "Where are the Barra biting at the moment?" was far more common when our man from Roper River was talking to our man at Mataranka. Mataranka is the next town due west of Roper River on the highway leading to Katherine and is a popular little town, famous for its hot springs.

One of my best mates who, unfortunately is not with us any more, was the lone CIB man for Katherine. His full name was Patrick Joseph Egerton Murphy, and he wasn't an Irishman, he was born in England, but spent most of his years in Rhodesia as it was known then. Charlie Taylor was our lone man at Timber Creek which is due west again from Katherine almost on the West Australia border where the Barramundi are very plentiful. Charlie was there for many years and was well known for the best catches of Barramundi on a very light line and, in fact, held a number of world records for his feats. He was a well-known and very capable outback policeman and he was always on time on his radio schedules.

When it was necessary to go to any of the missions up north on any of the islands, it was purely a matter of chartering a plane at the airport and flying out there for as long it took to solve the problem. Most of the problems on the northern missions related to fighting, theft or alcohol. The majority of the missions were run by the Uniting Church, and consequently there was a complete ban on alcohol.

The wet season in and around Darwin could be either a help or a hindrance, rarely was it both together. About 9am one morning my sergeant came to chat, and I could tell he had something on his mind. Eventually he said that he needed three or four people to fly out to

Numbulwar Mission, on the Gulf of Carpentaria, as they had a problem getting a fellow to Darwin. He was already in custody and just needed picking up and transporting back to Darwin. As well as that the sergeant required one of our ladies to take a statement from a complainant at the Catholic Mission at Roper, and also pick up some articles from the Roper River police station. He said that I needed to go to supervise these requirements and we would be back in a few hours' time, about 3pm or 4pm that same day.

There was no reason to take extra clothes or the like to satisfy that fellow called Justin (case). I attempted to explain that the wet season was unpredictable and we needed to cover certain matters in case (him again) we got held up somewhere and we were unable to return that afternoon. The sergeant would not listen to my plea and he handed me the necessary documents for the trip and went off back to his office.

I found Maree and my partner and told them the requirements of the trip and we went to the airport. We were fortunate that the only plane available was to be piloted by John Harding who I had flown with on a number of occasions, and I regarded him highly to make the trip safely with no problems. As was usual at that time of the year, the weather forecast was not good and afternoon storms were predicted. We flew out over Arnhem Land in heavy cloud and headed south-east towards the Roper River. John said that he had flown this way, but not in heavy cloud and asked had I been this route before on the ground. I was able to say yes I had, and I believed that any hills or the like would be no more than 500 feet high. He asked would I steer the plane whilst he did some instrument calculations. I gladly agreed and we continued on whilst he did his figures and I flew the plane with plenty of 'encouragement' from the two rear seats. We flew on for about ten minutes more and, at a height of 450 feet, came out of the cloud right over the top of Roper River. There were big cheers from our back seat passengers. We flew on for about 20 minutes and landed at the Roper River Catholic Mission, where we let Maree off and told her we would pick her up again in approx. three hours' time.

We took off again and shortly after takeoff ran into a rather rough storm with plenty of rain and severe winds which tossed our little Cessna round like a sheet of paper. John did not seem to worry, as he explained he had done it all before in New Guinea for a number of years. When we arrived in Numbulwar we got the paperwork done in a short time and headed off again. By this time it appeared that the storm had passed, which it had. But it had also dropped a lot of rain on the area we were going to land at, and both places where we had intended to land were flooded. Whilst we could have landed, we could not have taken off again till the following morning, providing there was no further rain, which was only guesswork anyway.

We radioed our situation though to Katherine and, after calculating that we had enough fuel to get to Katherine, decided to head for there. We felt sorry for Maree, who didn't even have a clean pair of knickers or any spare clothes at all. As we flew on towards Katherine we encountered another storm which we flew straight through. It was a bit rough but not as bad as earlier in the day. After refueling we headed north for Darwin and encountered a third storm that we again flew straight through and shortly afterwards a flashing red light on the dashboard activated.

John expressed his dismay but said it was an indicator that the undercarriage was not down or something was malfunctioning. On approach to Darwin he radioed the tower and requested a visual check of the undercarriage. The answer from the tower was good as they informed us that in fact it was down but they could not guarantee it was locked. We found out later that it was merely a faulty warning light. I never had a problem flying in any sort of weather after that experience. Our aboriginal offender and my offsider were both shaking like a leaf, and the former had gone a strange shade of green. To John, our pilot it was just another day at the office.

Whilst my memory serves me I shall try and relate to you a few other experiences I had flying during the wet season. Whilst there were other pilots available, it seemed that John was just waiting for me to call so that we could experience other unusual ways of handling the wet season in our little Cessna 337 Skymaster.

We were asked to fly across to Melville Island to deliver some goods to the Administrator and also to investigate a couple of break-ins to the offices there.

This turned out to be the easy part, as the people we were dealing with had been taught never to tell a lie. It was just a matter of getting a group of them together and asking 'Who dunnit', to which I received the reply, 'It was me boss'.

Whilst we were there a storm came through and dropped some very heavy rain right on the Garden Point airstrip from where we were intending to take off. The airstrip had just been graded and the residue which consisted of gravel and mud had been spread over the area. When we arrived it was quite dry but now it consisted of six inches of mud with our little plane stuck right in the middle. Even the props of the plane revving at almost full revs could not shift it, so we did the obvious thing, got out the shovels and dug it out. With the props going and more digging we managed to get it to the side of the strip where the gravel and mud had been graded from, which left us no more than the width of the undercarriage to use for take off. However, John, the good pilot that he was, reckoned that it if it was wide enough to fit the undercarriage, it was wide enough to take off. There was a young man who had been working at the mission who had decided to fly back with us, but he 'chickened out' when he saw how we were intending to take off. It was only a short strip in length, and we used every inch of it and headed for Darwin - in fact we were early, getting back at our estimated time.

Another adventure was to Wave Hill, where there is a Police Station and not much else, but there is a store of sorts that is run by the local police man, and also an airstrip. The store is a place where you order in what is required for the next three months or so, and you either pick it up from there or it is delivered to you (but only if the local man is heading your way). On this particular day we flew in to get the local policeman to sign some documents in relation to a court hearing which was getting close, and then fly out again and back to Darwin. John was again my pilot and he had never been to Wave Hill, and neither had I. We had been informed that it was a short runway, but it was very short. We did a fly over before landing and John said he was unsure whether it was long enough to land the plane but he managed it with quite a bit of runway to spare. John, who was never doubtful about his flying ability, stated that he barely had room to take off. However, after revving the engines with the brakes on, away we went and cleared the creek bed at the end by a few metres.

After a period I was teamed up with a guy who became my partner for the next few years. His name was Ewan Mackintosh and we worked together very well, handling most of the fraud cases such as bad cheques and petty crimes which were very prominent round the town at that time. Later, together with Sgt John Maley, I became part of the very first Northern Territory Drug Squad, and I was credited with having the first conviction for possession of marijuana. It consisted of a plant in a pot on the balcony of a block of units. The female offender was let off with a caution when she transferred the load of evidence to her boyfriend, who worked on the drilling rig near Broome. He broke a branch off it when he came home, then when he finished, she broke a few limbs off him for leaving it there on the balcony not knowing exactly what it was.

It was about mid June when Sgt. Goody approached me and asked me to go to Adelaide to do Detective Training School at the Adelaide Police Academy (known as Fort Largs) for a 5 week course, together with

Doug Hovey. Fort Largs was situated on the northern side of Glenelg Beach, walking distance to the main shopping district of that area and couple of kilometers to downtown Adelaide. Fort Largs was an old building that had been revamped, but the main building had been rebuilt to modern standards. Doing this Training School was difficult from the point of view that it was the middle of winter in South Australia and we both had to scratch around to get some warm clothes to wear. However, we managed to get enough to wear between us. Fortunately we were both much the same size.

Doug was an interesting fellow who had a very dry sense of humour. On one occasion he was helping out one of the local football clubs with a fundraising venture by looking after the money raised. Little did he know that at another part of the premises they were having a fund-raising in the form of a gambling night. Unfortunately Sgt. Goody got to hear about it but only the gambling part which Doug had nothing to do with. Sgt. Goody asked for an immediate report on the matter. He always liked the reports he received to commence with the phrase 'I have to report etc. etc.' so Doug wrote his report saying 'I have to report I have nothing to report'. The Sergeant had nothing he could do about it.

Around this time Joy and I had a visit from Maureen and her friend Gwen, who were the nurses from the girls' home when I was stationed at Burwood in Melbourne. Maureen found out we were going on leave a few weeks hence, and asked us if we would call and see her boyfriend to talk him into joining the Police Force in Darwin. About three months later Darryl Manzie joined the Force and went straight to the traffic branch. He married Maureen and they still live there to this day. Darryl was a very community minded person and he eventually became a member of the NT Parliament. Because of his police background he was appointed Attorney General, a post he held for number of years. He presently runs a talk back radio show in Darwin, is Australian President of the Dragon Boat Association, and over a period of time has been attached to a number of like organizations. For those of you who have not recognized his name, he was attorney-general over the whole period of the Lindy Chamberlin case. He had his own opinion on the situation and vowed that she would not get any compensation during his term in office.

The centenary of 100 years of policing in the Northern Territory was held in Alice Springs in April 1988 and the person who made the original finding as Coroner was a man named Dennis Barrett, whom you may recall, was my Sergeant at Fitzroy police station. Dennis, Darryl and myself sat down over a beer or two and did a lot of reminiscing over all aspects of the Lindy Chamberlin case, other cases, the present government, policemen we knew and whether the beer we were drinking was hot, cold or whatever. When you have had a few it doesn't really matter.

One day in Darwin, Ewan and I got a call from the Big W store to say that they had apprehended a shoplifter. We attended and were introduced to a middle aged well-groomed lady who had a jovial manner. Her manner of speech immediately questioned how this person could be a common shoplifter. We went into the office and the attendant showed us some items of ladies apparel that she had walked out of the store with. She stated before being questioned that she had merely had a lapse of memory and walked out without paying as she was thinking about something else at the time.

We were inclined to believe her as she said it happened but there was something about this lady that I had a strange feeling about. So I decided to drive her to her house in Fannie Bay to inspect her home, much to my partner's protests that it was a waste of time. By the time we got closer to her home address she was starting to fidget and could not sit still. We then realized that there was a lot more to this lady than she was telling us. She refused to give us the key to her apartment and refused to open the door. After a stern conversation she finally did so. We were absolutely stunned and amazed as we entered, as she ran around and closed all the doors and cupboards. An inspection of the whole of the unit, revealed hundreds and possibly thousands of items of women's clothing, shoes, dresses, jackets, souvenirs, jewelry, sheets, pillows and slips and many and varied items that are too numerous to mention. There were too many to fit in a standard size utility and required a second trip to gather it all together with the passenger seat piled high as well.

We took the liberty of checking the lady's bank accounts, and found that she had not drawn any funds out except for rent, but we also found that a lot of funds had been paid in. These we later found out were monies she had received for goods she had sold back to the merchants she stole them from, still with dockets attached, saying they would not fit or some similar story. We then had the tedious task of finding out who owned all the property. With the help of two policewomen who were a bit more adept at finding anything to do with women's clothing, it was surprising how quickly we cleared it, and we had as many complainants as we needed to go to court.

Of course we had to find somebody to go to court or we would have to let her go free. The matter was heard by the local magistrate's court and she was found guilty as charged, and sentenced to one month's jail wholly suspended due to her good behavior over that period. Because of the value of the stolen goods we could have opted for a higher court hearing but to get the value of the goods and the complainant for every item, and get them to court, would be more trouble than it was worth. I managed to contact every state in the country and did not find anything under her name or similar action.

Some months later I was reading the daily paper from Adelaide where a 54 year old woman had been charged with shoplifting and they had found lots of goods, similar to our lady friend here. I made a phone call to Adelaide and found out it was the same lady we had had here, and it was only her second conviction anywhere. During my years as a policeman I encountered many people who had the problem of stealing articles that they could ill afford. But their ego told them to walk out with an article without paying so they could brag to friends of like ilk, and by doing so achieve a very high status.

One person who achieved a status that was hard to beat, particularly as far as goods in a large quantity were concerned, was Raymond John White*. He became quite notorious in police circles and also in as far as the Government was concerned, when he discovered that the public in general were very keen on a fish called barramundi. He discovered that not only did members of the public like to catch them but they mainly liked to eat them. So he became the 'go to' man of the Department of Fisheries and it gave him control over quantities, length and daily catches, etc.. But it did not give him control over himself, and he became a very frequent fisherman in the Mary River wetlands where a catch of a utility load of fish was not uncommon. 99% of these were caught in his nets, which of course was illegal, and of course, he helped make the laws that made it illegal.

One late afternoon Ewan and I were informed it was our duty the following day to go out to the wetlands and catch him with illegally caught barramundi. We arrived at the wetlands at about 5am and there were 2 suspect vehicles present. The first one was a visitor from Adelaide, who had caught two large Barra's with a rod and line and was entitled to be there. So we concentrated our efforts on the second vehicle, which was the man we were looking for. We noted that man was by himself with a utility full of fish and nets and was trying to hide his illegal activity but he was a bit late cleaning up. It was good that we were able to find him so quickly. At this stage whilst trying to find the route out, we got ourselves bogged down but fortunately it was his track out and he wasn't going anywhere until we moved. At this stage he did not know who we were so I jumped into the passenger seat of his vehicle and Ewan drove ours until we got to the main road out. It was then I told him he was under arrest for illegal fishing. He had all sorts of stories that he said would exonerate him and leave us with egg on the face. However, he had numerous prior convictions, and the magistrate hearing the case was not impressed and sentenced him to six months in Fannie Bay Gaol.

Another matter that came to hand was a visitor to Darwin who decided that this town was fair game to pass a few valueless cheques, which were still in frequent use in those days. He in fact had more than a few outstanding, the value of which was close to a $1000 dollars. We made a few enquiries and finally located him at the Koala Motel where he had also issued a cheque for payment of his accommodation. He had also cashed a cheque for an amount of $400, covincing them that he was a high falootin' business man who had plenty of expense money to flash around whilst he was in town for a week. He also convinced them not to cash the cheque as he had just opened an account with the Darwin Commonwealth Bank, who had told him all funds would be ready in seven days.

Our enquiries at the bank showed no details that he had ever held an account there. When confronted by Ewan and I he said that there should be enough funds in his bank to cover any cheques he had written as he had only just opened the account there. When he was told that he was not known at the bank he said that it didn't matter as he could provide enough funds to cover all the cheques he had written. He excused himself for a moment or two when he went to his bedroom and came out in possession of a cheque book and proceeded to write some cheques. I then told him he was under arrest for fraud and he accompanied us to the police station. After delving into his past we discovered that the cheque book was stolen from a person in Alice Springs and he only intended to use it until the cheques ran out. After checking his background we found that he had numerous convictions for cheque offences over a lengthy period of time. The magistrate described him as a blot on society and gave him a small taste of Fannie Bay Gaol for 3 months.

There was one period where it was relatively quiet round the town and Ewan and I were just doing a general patrol and having a look around some of the past hot spots round the town. We received a radio message from the city asking if there was anyone in the vicinity of the Narrows to take a reasonably urgent call. We were in the Narrows at the time so I took the call. We were also asked if we had a firearm so I requested details of the location and the home of the complainant. Having that information we realized we knew the complainant and her husband well, so we said that we would take the call as the complainant and her husband were known to us through past domestic disputes.

We went to the door and knocked, and the door opened to a man with a big revolver in his right hand, I dived straight at him and flattened him to the floor and crashed through the partition surrounding the front door. The gun meanwhile had fallen to the floor and Ewan had grabbed it. He then examined it and found it to be unloaded and also found it to be a replica. We spoke to his wife who had been told it was only a toy. However, we were unaware at the time that it was only a replica. Ewan asked what was next. My reply was, "I need a drink".

The house we were by then living in had been allocated by the NT government. We were most impressed by the quality of the accommodation. It was a three bedroom home built on pylons with the laundry and storeroom underneath the upstairs bathroom and toilet, and there was room to park two vehicles underneath. We were provided with the house free of charge but there was a very small charge for the provision and use of furniture and whitegoods. The underneath section of the home was useful for many things which included building a yacht. This yacht was an 18ft Fletcher design with a single mast and enclosed cabin and had a drop keel that was adjustable, for stability. Quite a few of the materials to complete the building of the craft were supplied, and included the plans. The hull was almost complete and included the fibreglassing, and the windows just had to be slotted into place once the main part of the hull was complete. The sails were also supplied, which were standard fitting for the boat. The builder also supplied a massive headsail that was actually too big for my boat but when testing it later when it was finished, we found it was very useful when we entered in Club races. Results were consistent with the amount each boat carried and the handicap was adjusted accordingly.

Each year they had a Darwin to Gunn Point Race that was an overnight jaunt where you slept on the boat and raced back to Darwin the following morning. I awoke about 5am the next day to find Max, my crewman, engineer, and whatever you want done sort of bloke, sitting on the rocks quite close to our mooring, eating oysters off the rocks with a knife. We finally got going when the other boats could be seen just disappearing over the horizon.

The ride home was quite different particularly as we had a following wind. Max really did know how to sail and the whopping big headsail really proved its worth when we rigged it up like a kite, or a spinnaker to the uninitiated. In fact after about an hour and a half we were almost in front, and a further half hour we were a few hundred yards in front. The other sailors were starting to get agitated as Max kept sailing across their bows and taking the wind from their sails. However, by the time we got through the channel next to Bathurst Island and into Darwin Harbor we were running second last and by the time the racing committee had done their handicapping, and had worked out that we were not properly equipped for racing (which we knew),

18' Fletcher designed yacht

they agreed that our boat was very fast. There was a bit of jealousy involved but, all in all, it was a great weekend. There was a lot of interest in our boat once the dust had settled but most concluded that even when fully equipped for racing, and with the sails managed properly, there wasn't a boat that could beat her.

A few days later whilst sitting in the squad room my Sergeant, known as Billy the Good, came in and asked if I had ever been to Borraloola. Without his question answered, he further said he would like me to go there. In conjunction with the local policeman, David Moore, we would sort out the owner of a herd of cattle that had just come into his possession, with nobody claiming ownership at this stage. He said, with a big smile on his face, that I had better go home and get organized and load up a vehicle with all the necessaries as I could be away for a few days.

I did as he requested and was ready to leave at about 5am the following morning to drive about 900k to what is commonly known by the locals as The Loo. I also took the liberty of taking one of the two-way radios. The radios were ex-army sets and they were very user friendly. All you had to do was toss the aerial wire over the branch of a tree, and you could transmit to either Darwin or Alice Springs. Rather handy when you are right out in the scrub country. The power they operated on was 12volt, so that was handy as well as they just clipped to the car battery.

I arrived at Daly Waters at about 1pm and called in at the local police station. I was informed that the local man had already left to go to The Loo to help keep control of the cattle, of which there was over a hundred head. I was also informed that he had his aboriginal tracker with him as he was known as a very good stockman. I arrived at 'The Loo' at about 4.30pm, and noted many head of cattle fenced into a temporary yard with two aboriginal stockmen on horseback attempting to keep them all together. We had a meeting and concluded that the best temporary solution was to make sure the cattle remained in the yard, so we built some temporary fences fronting on to the large lagoon nearby. If they wished to drink some water they could do so and would be less likely to attempt to break out of the compound.

We noted that they were all wearing new brands made by using three separate branding irons. This was unusual as the normal method would be to use one iron with the three letters on it. I radioed Darwin and requested they look in the brands register and find out who owned the brand, which appeared to only have been used in the previous week. We did find out that the brand belonged to the Elizabeth Downs Station but was only for their top stud cattle and the brands were triple letters on a single branding iron and had not been used for at least nine months. The cattle that we had yarded were what they called scrubbers, and station management stated the cattle we had yarded did not belong to them and they weren't interested in them.

Constable David Moore said that he had found out that the stockmen from Elizabeth Downs were presently doing a muster north from Wollagorang adjacent to the backwaters of the Gulf of Carpentaria, about 150ks away. We decided to go and meet up with them to get a statement to write off ownership of the cattle we were holding. We crossed the McArthur River and headed east along the main road connecting 'The Loo' to Wollagorang, located the head stockman and he was able to state that these cattle did not belong to them.

We then headed back again but approximately half way we ran across a boulder in the road when negotiating a bend and our ute turned over on its side. We eventually managed to right it again with the help of a few boulders and a hydraulic jack. We restarted and drove on, fortunately with no injuries and a very small amount of damage, but knowing it would take a mountain of paper work to rectify the ute. We nearly lost it again when crossing the river at about a three-quarter tide and we were just able to cross it with about ten minutes to spare, otherwise we would have been there for about 6 hours waiting for the tide to change.

We had been back about ten minutes only when there was a knock on the door and I heard Dave say "Well hello, just the man we have been waiting for, we have a problem with some cattle, we can't find owners for". He showed this man into the office and introduced him as James Morris*, Chairman of the NT Cattlemen's Association.

Dave Moore explained that he had a complaint a few days ago when a neighbor said that a whole herd of cattle had trampled and eaten his vegie patch from which he supplied a number of locals including Morris and his wife, for about the last two years. When he complained to Morris he was told to forget about it and grow them again next year. Dave Moore said that he had heard that Morris dealt in cattle and sent a truck load away every year. Moore said that it was only his second year at 'The Loo' and in that area people were spread out, so he had yet get to know everybody in the district. The neighbour said that Morris was the man we were looking for and he had heard a rumor that sometime in the next week a truck would arrive to pick up the cattle.

I decided that if he was under arrest he would be less likely to do a runner. I informed Morris of my decision and said he had a choice to behave and stay with us or misbehave and get locked in the local lock-up that gets very hot. I asked Morris about the truck and he said that it was due at 6pm that very afternoon. I radioed Darwin and was put through to Inspector Len Cossons, the CIB chief. I filled him in as to how this matter was going and where it was heading. I said that under the present circumstances I intended to photograph each beast in the herd then order a truck and transport them to Katherine. There they could be looked after for a few days pending getting Morris before a court either in Katherine or Darwin.

However, all that must have been too much for the inspector who then ordered me to round up the cattle and deliver them back to their rightful owner, and bring the offender back to Darwin. I suggested that it may be a good idea to truck the cattle to Katherine, mainly to keep them out of the reach of Morris's cronies who would be likely to interfere with them. When I told the inspector who we had arrested he said, "A man in his position would not do that, are you sure you have got the right man, you had better go and check".

About 30 mins later the truck arrived. It was a B Double livestock carrier and was capable of transporting 120 cattle. I obtained a statement from the truck driver/owner, who then drove off 'at a fast rate of knots'. It was suggested by Dave Moore that they could look after the cattle for a few days with the manpower they had. But there was the danger of the locals banding together to run the cattle off into the scrub, particularly as Morris' wife lived in the area and he was so well known.

'The Job' and Beyond

It was a long drive straight to Katherine but we got there before midnight. We had refreshments there and we were about to head off again when the Sergeant in charge of the night shift said that they had two of their members going to Darwin the following day for a court matter and suggested that they bring the prisoner to Darwin as it would be safer.

I agreed and headed for home on my own, arriving at home in the early hours of the morning. After a lengthy nap I called at the Inspector's office and he had already been in touch with Katherine whose members had transported Morris from there to Darwin. He started to berate me and tried to tell me what he would have done if he had been there. I interrupted and asked him if he had ever been to Borroloola. He said no he had not been there, but had been to that area and knew how to deal with the people who lived there. I told him I was unable to work under his command any longer. I asked him if I could be transferred back to the uniformed section. He said that would be easily arranged and organized it with a phone call on the spot.

I said that before I left we had better do something about the cattle we had yarded at Borroloola. He said, "Not a problem, I will do it now if you could give me a report on the whole matter". I told him I had done it and it was in his attention tray in his office. About a week later one of my former colleagues, Sgt. Alexander, called in to see me and said I should know that he had just returned from Borroloola and he could not find one thing I had done wrong. He had reported the same to Inspector Cossons. A day or two later the Inspector called to see me and reported that all the cattle had been run off into the scrub and it was a case of 'no cattle - no case'. Unfortunately he was not the sort of person who could ever offer an apology.

Joy's father, who was also a policeman in Victoria, had decided to retire and drive around Australia but, as his wife was not able to travel such long distances by car, she came to stay with Joy and myself in Darwin while he did the trip with one of his buddies. He was most impressed with the facilities provided by the NT Government on our behalf and he was most impressed by the yacht I was building. Vic Hetherington, a retired Victorian Policeman was capable of doing anything he desired. He was a builder, a motor mechanic and Jack of all Trades. He could do anything well and was a perfectionist. If he didn't know how to do something, he would figure it out by the following day. If you couldn't buy it, he would make it. Before he retired from the Victoria Police he took over the police station at Marysville which, in the 2009 Black Saturday bush fires, was burnt out and many lives were lost. Vic had long since retired. Once when we were visiting from the NT, the telephone rang one evening and he was required to attend the scene of a car accident a few miles away. He asked me to accompany him to the scene that consisted of a single vehicle that had run off the road. The driver stated that he didn't know the road well and been blinded by a vehicle coming from the opposite direction. Vic later said that it had worked out fine with me doing the paperwork as he said he disliked the paperwork associated with vehicle accidents.

Some weeks after the cattle incident a vacancy came to my attention for a replacement to the CIB team at Alice Springs, so naturally enough I gave it some serious thought but realized that it still came under the control of Inspector Cossons, whom I vowed I would not work for again. So I sought the attention of my current boss, Sergeant Andy McNeill, and informed him that I intended to resign my position with the NT Police and return to Victoria. I also informed him that I would prefer to resign on my own terms as I had quite a few cases pending, and I did not wish to keep returning just for the outstanding court matters.

Sgt. McNeill agreed that about six weeks would be sufficient to clear them. He said that it would also give me time to catch up with some of the friends I had made over the few years I had been there. The following day he called me into his office and said there hadn't been a patrol to Arnhem Land for a while, and there were quite a few things that needed attention. He also suggested that I take a new man with me to show him the ropes, that man being Constable Alan La Porte, who was very new to the job. As he was dark skinned, we thought he would get on well with our indigenous population. Upon meeting Alan he informed me he inherited his looks from his French father and African mother. I informed him that we will probably be away for a few days, so he better find out about sleeping on the ground in a swag, as we will be heading off in a day or two. We decided to leave early the following morning so I picked up Alan at HQ. He was just finishing off a little paper work that was required for a court matter the day after that, when we would have been away.(Now there you go he's learning already.)

We headed south and then turned east along the main drag to Jim Jim in the north and Jabiru in the south. We caught up with some guys at Jabiru, and fixed up the paper work regarding some car ownership and registration details, which was all done by the local police in those days (but apparently not correctly).

We continued on and then north towards the Jim Jim Hotel and en-route passed the caravan and campsite of Wayne Cubis, who was a former police officer who left the service and joined the Dept. of Fisheries where (his words) he lived a life of luxury and splendor, with home grown barramundi every day for breakfast, and dinner as well if he wished. It certainly was the place to catch Barramundi as we found out shortly after.

As we were travelling down a track which hadn't been used for quite a while, I spotted a small lagoon that I had not seen before on trips through the area. I got the fishing rods out and went down to the edge of the lagoon and caste a lure into the waters where there was lots of vegetation. There was an immediate hit on the lure and a large barramundi tossed the lure back to me. I cast it again and the fish hit it again and I was able to reel it in the second time. We travelled south again towards Wayne's campsite and found he had just arrived home. When he questioned as to where I had caught the fish, I was informed that that particular lagoon was out of bounds to fishing. However he said that the fish was now dead and he would put it in his freezer for when we were returning. It weighed in at 9.2 lbs.

We decided on an overnight stay at Mudginberri Station where they always have a spare room in the staff quarters for travelling police. This station is one of the most picturesque places in the Northern Territory and is built next to a large lagoon. It faces south east onto the lagoon with escarpments surrounding it in a half circle. Travelling police are invited to take advantage of the facilities which included beds, bed linen, breakfast and even the use of a dingy if I wished to go fishing in the morning. A staff member was sighted fishing in the morning and was able to catch two large barramundi, which he literally tossed on the barbie, cooked up and invited other staff to share with him. Alan had not tasted barramundi cooked with such simplicity and tasting so nice.

We were notified by management that Constable La Porte was required back at Darwin and they would send a man out to take his place. About two hours later Constable Bryce Fardell arrived, and Alan La Porte drove back to Darwin albeit with at least some experience of the area now known to him. I kept in touch with Bryce Fardell as we both had similar investigation businesses, which had been established upon leaving the Northern Territory Police, and we were able to help each other out.

A couple of weeks later I was packed up and ready to leave the Territory and we decided to drive the first section at night, which was not the best decision I've ever made. About an hour and a half out of Darwin and close to the Bachelor turn-off, a large scrub bull walked casually across the road in front of the car, only about ten meters away, which gave me no time to stop. The left hand front of the car struck the beast on its right shoulder and head, which killed it instantly, whilst the rear wrapped around the left side of car, doing very little damage to either the left hand side of the car or the front, but it broke all the lights on the left side. Janine, who was about four years old at the time, was asleep on the rear seat and packed amongst the luggage.

My reliable old Peugeot stood up well and had it been any other car, one or all of the family may have been injured. A short time later the policeman from Bachelor arrived at the scene and suggested it may be a good idea if we stayed with him overnight and sort things out in the morning. We did that and returned to

Darwin the next day. I managed to get flights home for the family, and I drove home once the car was repaired. My good friend Bill Miller offered me accommodation for the interim period for which I was most grateful. Bill was on the committee of the Waratah Sports Club and was inclined to stay on at the club of an evening particularly when he had a little too much to drink. His wife Beth decided to do something about it, so she got some plain sticky tape and placed it over the front and back door locks. When Bill arrived home after a few and also a few more, could not find the lock to get his key in, nor could he find the rear one. He banged on the doors, the windows, and everywhere, but could not get his key to open anything. He finished up sleeping in his car that night, and from then on he was very punctual on arriving home for dinner. Good one Beth.

BACK IN MELBOURNE

After arriving back in Melbourne, we stayed at my mother's place in Mitcham where Joy easily found a teaching job at the local Catholic School. Whilst my mother was quite an astute person, I must have failed in that subject as it was my mother who found a newspaper advert with somebody wanting to hire a person with a security background. I rang the number connected to the advert and I spoke only long enough to get the details from him and he suggested that he come and talk to me in person. When he arrived he introduced himself as Geoffrey Hossack of Security Pacific, Punt Road, South Yarra. He stated that he always did his interviews at his employee's premises as it gave him a better idea of the person he was employing.

My employment consisted of many hours of surveillance over a period of a few days to gather evidence of insurance fraud, plus a walkthrough of a large lingerie factory in North Melbourne, the same or similar for a large carpet factory in Preston, and various other businesses that needed attention to guard them from inside and outside theft. These duties were performed with great enthusiasm. Unfortunately there was a lot of theft by employees who knew the workings of the factories and knew how to get goods out the door without being noticed.

One day I received a phone call from Geoff saying that one of his regular customers was having some difficulties with a man from Belgium who was caretaking a large complex where eels were bred, grown, and marketed to Japan on a fortnightly basis. However, the caretaker/manager had been running his own little business on the side, and the regular business was not performing as expected. The object of the exercise was to send someone down there to look after the farm whilst the manager was called to Melbourne office where he would be sacked. It was feared that if he was left there he would pull the plug and we would find what was left of the ponds with no eels in them. I was asked to go there and remain overnight in case this happened when he came home from Melbourne.

The company also owned a gold mine, about two hours away, and they sent one of their employees from there also to keep me company and to act as a back-up. My off-sider arrived at 7pm and he was driving an old Holden that he described as his home as it contained everything he owned. We noted that a car arrived at about 10.30pm and drove through to the house at the rear of the ponds. About half an hour later the manager came with a dog to the area where we were and we had a short conversation about our presence there and what we required him to do. He ordered us to be gone by the following morning or to suffer the consequences.

The following morning he came to the area where we were camped and demanded we move and, when we refused, he said he would move us. He went across to where a medium size John Deere bulldozer was parked and started the engine. He drove across to where my off-sider's Holden was parked and put the blade under the front of it and pushed it about five metres. He then began to shift my new panel van. I made a quick decision and grabbed my double barrel shotgun from the rear of my car, walked around to the right hand side of the bulldozer and fired two shots into the injectors, stopping it immediately. Our Belgian man jumped off the Dozer and ran to his house yelling he would ring the police. Fortunately he had not done any damage to my vehicle and only minor damage to my off-sider's car. The police arrived about an hour later and had a quick chat to me, then went to see our caretaker man and informed him that, if he was no longer required at the eel farm, he was now trespassing and it would be in his best interest to leave as soon as possible. I radioed this information to Geoff and he arrived about two hours later. As Geoff drove down the track into the eel farm he had his VHF radio going really loud. It was playing, "I shot the Sherriff".

CHIRNSIDE PARK

Once in Melbourne we decided to build a house and spent many hours looking at various areas. We finally bought a corner block of land in Chirnside Park, adjacent to Lilydale and Mooroolbark, on the high side of the street facing north east and looking straight down the 6th fairway of the golf course. My brother Glyn was an architect and he offered to design a house that fitted the land and the area. He designed a house that was 34 squares with 3 bedrooms, ensuite, parents' retreat and bathroom upstairs, and a study, family room, kitchen/dining area and a formal dining room with room for a bar on the lower floor. The house consisted of five levels and was a solid brick home incorporating 42,000 bricks.

Joy and I became the owner/builders and Joy's father became the builder-extraordinaire. Years later a large extension and bathroom facilities were added which brought the size of the house to 42 squares. We recruited Jim Ellis as our plumber and Stan Balle became the drainage and excavator. Jim was a tradesman to be the envy of all tradesmen. When he had finished it was not possible to find where he had been working as he was extremely tidy. Both Jim and Stan became firm friends for the following years.

Eventually this home became our first office for Arrow Investigations. We used it for a number of years

'The Job' and Beyond

before moving to an office in Main Street, Lilydale. The business grew larger over a fairly short time span and the move into the office was very necessary as we needed somewhere for the employees to finish their paperwork during late afternoon.

At that time, I also joined the Chirnside Park Country Club and played golf there whenever time permitted. I played off a handicap of 15 but could not reach the magical single figures. At one point I came down to 12.6 but could not hold it and quickly went back to my comfort zone of 15. I became involved with the administration side of the Club and held the position of Vice President for a number of years, under the guidance of Ray Andrews. Ray worked in Melbourne so it became very convenient for him to phone me if there was an urgent problem at the Club, as I was only a few minutes away in Lilydale. This happened on a fairly regular basis. As a result of one of these problems I found it necessary to request that the then lady secretary, take over as secretary/manager. This turned out to be an outstanding decision, as the lady still holds the position today and has recently reached over 30 years of employment. This Lady is Barbara Kelly, who is one of the most sought after people in that position in the State of Victoria, and possibly Australia. I eventually took over as President of the Club and served for 2 years.

During this period of our business we took a trip with the children to the West Coast of the USA, including Disneyland. Later, Darryl decided he wished to go back to the States to play tennis and put all his efforts into achieving that aim. His mother and I made the decision that he should be given the opportunity as it appeared he had the ability and determination. He attended a Tennis Camp in Geelong, run by John Newcomb and

Tony Roche, which confirmed in his own mind he was good enough, particularly after playing against Pat Cash on one occasion.

After sending resumes to a number of colleges in various parts of the States, he received a message from Coach Herring of DeKalb College in Atlanta, Georgia that there was a position on his team and it was open for Darryl if he wished to take it up. It was a two year stint and seemed a great opportunity for him and for us to further our travels to the USA. We never at any stage anticipated that two years would turn into four years, and then a lifetime and career in the United States for Darryl. He played Division 1 college tennis and competed successfully in both local and regional USTA tournaments. After college he took up a position with the USTA as a Schools Director and over-saw schools in four of the southern states, teaching educators ways that they could utilize the facilities and equipment they had, be it large or small, and teaching kids to have fun playing tennis. He later took up coaching at a number of tennis clubs in Atlanta and also ran coaching clinics for all age groups, beginners to seniors, arranging for some well-known tennis players to assist on the day. It was a big thrill for us to meet Billie-Jean King on one of these days held whilst we were visiting.

On another of our trips Janine and my mother, Edna travelled with us and we decided to go via England, catch up on a bit of ancestry and visit where my mother grew up. She was now 79 and recalled that she had left the docks at Plymouth, England in 1926 and migrated to Oz with her family and had not returned until we travelled north to Manchester. We stayed overnight at a little English Pub, then the next day located her old home and school which were both in the same village.

However, the highlight of her visit was visiting her best friend Bessy, who had waved her goodbye at the docks so long ago when they were both 16 years old. We stayed on in England for a few days visiting a few different places such as Cardiff in Wales where my father was born, London and the sights surrounding it, and then off to Gatwick International airport from where we flew out to the USA, landing at Miami. Then it was on to one of the biggest airports in the world known as Hartsfield Jackson in Atlanta, Georgia where Darryl was waiting to drive us to a unit in Roswell that we had rented and where we stayed for the next six weeks.

From there we did quite a bit of sight-seeing throughout Georgia and the neighbouring states, had an amazing time and eventually thought about heading for home as my mother was getting a little weary. She normally travelled for a maximum of about a week and the long holiday was starting to get the better of her. We said goodbye to Darryl and eventually arrived home to find that Denise, our secretary, had everything under control and there was absolutely nothing left to do. From there on in I called her "The World's Greatest Secretary".

Perhaps the most memorable of our trips was in December 2011 to Virginia, where Darryl was Director of Tennis at Wintergreen Resort. We spent a wonderful white Christmas with Darryl, Julie and family and were also joined by Janine, Ian and the girls. This was the first time that the children had met and they spent many happy hours ski-ing on the adjacent snowfields connected to the resort and enjoying each other's company. The golf component of the resort was at the bottom of the mountain in the little town of Nellysford which Darryl described as being 'a one horse town that had forgotten the horse'.

Darryl has now been living and working in the United States for 37 years and, amongst other awards, has been recognized by the USPTA as a Master Professional, a designation held by only 150 of 15,000 professionals. Darryl has been Director of Tennis at Old Town Club, Winston-Salem NC since 2012. He and Julie have 3 children, Clarke, Connor and Katie and 3 grandchildren.

Meeting Bille-Jean King

ARROW INVESTIGATIONS

After working for Geoff Hossack for a number of years I left Security Pacific and started my own similar business but with more diversification. The new business was named Arrow Investigations and our motto was *"We Get Straight to the Point"*. We conducted surveillance on many persons cheating with Insurance Claims and took on a lot of work for some of the big law firms mostly in Melbourne. And for the latter part settled claims for the various Insurance Companies, wishing to clear their books of cumbersome claims which for the most part were fraudulent anyway.

I also ran across an old acquaintance of mine being Dennis Barrett, who was the sergeant I worked under at Fitzroy Police Station who had left the service to do a Law Degree. He 'ordered me' to have lunch with him, as he had just been appointed Magistrate for Alice Springs and wished to know a little more about the police service in the Northern Territory. I told him what he needed to know and before long he was in the news anyway, as he was appointed Coroner for Alice Springs, and presided over the infamous Lindy Chamberlin matter which put his name up in lights and his verdict was the most sensible in the whole affair.

Most of our work where surveillance was involved concerned workplace injuries, and we were hired by the insurance companies to obtain evidence to refute what was put to them to enhance the evidence of the claimant. For some of these supposed claimants we used multiple vehicle surveillance to catch them out. Although photographic equipment is far more sophisticated these days, it is surprising what we could achieve. As far as the film we obtained to refute the claims, we regarded it with some pride, as we became very well known for the quality of evidence we put before the courts. In one case in the Melbourne Supreme Court I was asked by the judge why I told the claimant a lie, to which I replied, "I was searching for the truth, Your Honor".

We served anywhere between 3,000 to 5,000 summonses and documents per year, some years there were more than that. We did most of our work in this field for local government, where we served summonses for non-payment of rates. We eventually were serving for three different councils in the near area. In one particular incident, the recipient refused to accept service unless I sat and had a beer with him or until we finished off a 6-pack and providing I shouted him a beer the following year, which I said I would and did. I had two other services which were supposed to be difficult. The first one was on Frank Hardy, the well-known journalist and author, who lived in the Collingwood area but no one could find him. I managed to find him as a result of an article in a local magazine, where he described an old chimney stack as his only view. I found the chimney stack, and subsequently Frank Hardy, and he wasn't pleased.

The second one was organized through one of my client's lawyers and it involved a solicitor arriving on a plane from Sydney with a bundle of documents to be served on the Secretary of the Transport Workers Union, who said he would not accept service of any document in regard to a matter concerning the Federal Government and the Union. I picked up the young solicitor from the airport and drove to the Union Office at the top of Swanston Street. His receptionist said he would not be in for the rest of the day and she doubted he would be in the next day. I made a few discreet inquiries and then I took the solicitor and his bundle of documents to the 1st Floor Media room where they were just ready for a television interview. The lights came on, our man came out, the television cameras rolled and I walked up and served him with the documents. The solicitor stated that we were on national television and said, "I don't think we will even need an affidavit for that service".

On one of the days when I was out serving summonses on the council defendants, it was about 7pm in the evening and a man came to the door and it appeared he had had quite a bit to drink. After accepting the service he said to me, "Aren't you supposed to deliver these things between sunrise and sunset," to which I replied

"Not necessarily, 7pm is good don't you think?"

He replied, "Maybe I meant sunset and sunrise". He then closed the door holding the summons up and waved goodbye.

During, what we called our summons season, our secretary Denise Roberts set our summons up in piles in alphabetical and numerical order depending what was required. Our servers called in, grabbed a bundle and went out for the whole day just delivering (serving). One of our servers, David Whitworth, holds the record of 98 in one day, a great effort when you are aware what was required. The Lillydale Shire Council (now called Yarra Ranges) used a specialist legal firm to make out and print the summonses before they came to us and all we did was charge the council a small fee for the service. The CEO of the rates department asked me if we would be interested in teaching them how to make up the summons so they could make them up themselves. We would charge them a little more on each summons for the privilege of teaching them how to make them up. I did the sums on it and readily agreed to do it. Apparently they also had a 'too hard basket' where the summons had built up over a number of years. I asked if they would like me to attempt to serve them to which they readily agreed. We managed to serve 78 per cent of the outstanding documents.

HERVEY BAY

In May 1988 we travelled to the Gold Coast to visit and attend Expo 88 which had been available for viewing for about three months. After Expo we continued on to Hervey Bay to visit some of my best friends from Police days, being Roy and Claire Beasley formerly of Warrandyte, a suburb of Melbourne, adjoining Lilydale. Roy is aforementioned in this text as Constable Roy Beasley of Burwood. He was quite adamant that Hervey Bay was going places and real estate would be quite valuable in the near future. We made contact with the principle of Ray White real estate who offered to show us around, looking at vacant land, buildings and commercial premises with businesses operating on them.

We looked at a putt-putt business on a three quarter acre block of land one street from the beach front. We looked at many others but decided to buy this block and the business combined for what we considered was a very reasonable price. We were quite aware that the business was not operating to its best potential and there was a need for some work to be done if or when we took it over. The business operated on a 12 months lease with no further options, and in fact the lease had nearly run out by the time the purchase of the land had been finalised. The operators said that they wished to continue on a month by month basis, regardless of what our wishes were, and they said quite emphatically that there was little we could do about it whilst we were in Melbourne. They found out a lot more about it when I turned up at the premises 18 hours later and very nicely said it was time they departed, as the monthly lease that they had dreamed up had expired and they had three days to vacate the premises.

My good mate Roy offered to look after and clean up the property until we could finalize our business in Melbourne. We sold our house in Croydon easily, and moved to Hervey Bay and a new era in our lives commenced. We became Golf and Games. We also bought an old Queenslander in Point Vernon and decided to leave the tenants in the house and lived in our caravan which was a lot closer to the business. These tenants were a lot more agreeable and rented the premises for a number of years before eventually buying it from us. In the meantime a very large old Queenslander came up for sale almost opposite the business, which suited us admirably as from the front veranda we could see the business property.

After sitting at the kiosk at the putt-putt over the winter months and not seeing many customers, I decided to expand it by building a waterslide over the top of the mini-golf. I made a visit to the Hervey Bay Council and sought out the tourism councilor, a very affable man named Kenny Bennett, who immediately said he was willing to give us all the help we needed to build the slide. The local branch of the National Australia Bank also indicated they would get behind it by lending us some money (now there's a surprise) and after only one visit and one phone call.

The following four to six weeks were taken up looking at waterslides, checking out construction methods, swimming pools, filtration, safety procedures and, most importantly, Public Liability Insurance. By chance we found the remnants of a slide, which had previously been erected at Upper Mount Gravatt and had been left lying on the ground for some time. I managed to purchase 220 meters of waterslide in varied shapes and sizes, two very large electric motors, pumps and pump house equipment and also a switchboard for a little over $5000, which I considered to be a very good deal. It became an even better deal when I realised that we were only going to use approximately 130 meters and I was able to sell the remainder, also for $5000, and that amount was slide pieces only.

After about 4 months and a few setbacks, the structure was finally completed and it seemed only right that I should be the first slider to go down the slide, and break the ice (so to speak). I admit that I had never been on a waterslide before that day, and needless to say I was more than a little edgy.

We decided on an opening date of the first Saturday of the September school holidays of 1993 and, as is normal with these sort of projects, in trying to meet the obligations of the advertised opening day we still had some landscaping work to be completed as the first sliders went up the tower.

Over the ensuing years the business generated a steady influx of customers who came from not only local areas but from as far as 400 kms away including Brisbane and Ipswich, which were quite distant from Hervey Bay. A big portion of the custom was from school excursions, youth clubs, disabled groups, birthday parties, sporting teams for training purposes, plus many thousands of single patrons. We were fortunate to be able to obtain good staff who were conscious of the safety requirements on these type of businesses, and they had no hesitation in ejecting patrons who disobeyed the rules. We had many junior staff and two or three very valuable seniors, two that were particular standouts. One guy worked with us for the full period we had the business; his name was Paul Tapscott. Paul was a big fellow who was training to be a chef, so the times of operation suited him to a tee. He was the type of employee who was never idle, and when the slide was quiet for a short time he would grab a broom and do some tidying up and then quickly back to the pool when we had patrons on the slide. He was wonderful with small children, and treated them like his own.

The other one was a lady named Noelene Bower who was also a very conscientious employee and a bundle of laughs. She looked after the children on the slide as if they were her own and scolded them if they broke the rules. Quite often, well-endowed young girls would come down the slide and lose their bikini tops when they hit the water. I would get the message on the two way radio on the tower of, "White pointers in the pool, Al." Yes, personality means a lot when you are dealing with a lot of people at the one time.

As you can imagine by the text, it was a business which created a great deal of good will and fun and it was an asset to the local area. During the season and particularly during the school holiday periods, I started work at 6.00am and finally got home about 10.30pm whilst Joy started at 9am in the kiosk, on the till, and in the games room, plus meals for us, so we both worked the long hours together. Every business that runs machinery has a break down from time to time and on the rare times we had a breakdown it was nearly always electrical. So it was just a matter of ringing a fellow named Warwick Day-Lewis, electrician extraordinaire, and he was there within 10 minutes even in busy times. We always treated him well, which was very important, as he was running a business of his own. Over a period of time we were very lucky to create a reputation where people in the district knew they could drop their children off and leave them there, knowing that they would be well supervised.

One day I had a phone call asking if we would be open the following day for a group of people. Well, the next day they arrived with a large group of people, approximately 35 of them.

I jokingly said, "Did you bring the whole town?"

"As a matter of fact we did," he replied. I learned a little later that what he said was true and the only person they left home was the stationmaster to allow the trains to go through. In fact the town was a few houses that were owned by Qld Rail.

Another day we had a man come in and ask if a group could come early the next day to have their monthly meeting and, afterwards, use our facilities. I opened up early for them as a special gesture. They used our facilities, I think they meant the toilets, and departed without spending a cent. They were the local group from National Seniors and there were 22 of them. To give them the normal group discount for the mini-golf only they would have been looking at $3.00 each against a normal price of $5.00 each. But we noted over a period of time that seniors generally had a great time playing putt-putt golf, this particular group only had the meeting to keep them amused.

The difference was when we hosted the Maryborough Elderly Citizens group - it was a laugh a minute. I usually set up a few extra obstacles on the greens that caused a lot of laughs. I set up one green where the ball had to be hit backwards through the legs. The fellow who was in charge of the group asked me to read out the scores and insisted that I announce the scores on the particular green, which he called 'the between the legs green'. So, that was the difference between two groups of a similar age.

The local rugby union team used to come at least twice a season to train on the stairs of the waterslide and organize a time trial up the tower and down the slide in a specified time. We also had regulars on the waterslide and playing mini-golf. Most of them were family groups whilst others were children who had been dropped off by their parents to get them out of the parents' way for the day. One of those was named Lachlan, and I still shudder any time I hear that name mentioned. The Lachlan I mention was a 12 year old boy who, wherever he was and whatever he was doing or not doing, was breaking the rules, or committing a crime. Whatever he was told to do, he did the opposite and his mother, who dropped him off, was as uncooperative as he was and could not understand how we could possibly ban a boy of his age. My explanation to that was, "very easily". But the problem was keeping him out. One day I didn't see him coming in the gate but one of the sliders came and complained that there was a boy up there sitting in the tunnel. That was a very short assessment of Lachlan. It wasn't what he did or didn't do but he was more likely to cause another person to have an accident.

The worst or most costly part of the business was the public liability insurance which cost us over $12,000 per year. Apparently the insurance company sent a person or persons to our property to have a day out and assess how we ran our business, with a view to setting a starting price for the liability. Well we were obviously doing something right as they rang me a couple of days later to tell me we were spot on with the way we ran our business and as a consequence to that they would only charge us 50 per cent of the original price for the liability insurance.

I had a great interest in the local AFL team known as the Hervey Bay Bombers and I was the treasurer. At the same time I was also chairman of the Tribunal, however the two positions clashed and as a result it was declared that I would have to resign from the treasurer's position. About a week later I was asked if I would consider becoming chairman of the League, known as the Bundaberg Wide Bay Football League. At the next meeting of the league I agreed to take on the position, as long as I was permitted to do it my way. This was agreed.

At the time of me taking on the position the league had only four teams, two from Bundaberg, one from Hervey Bay and one from Maryborough, the latter being very weak and some weeks were struggling to field a team. As a result of these meetings I went to Brisbane and consulted the President of AFL Queensland, who promised to do a shuffle of teams so that we could enjoy the benefits of belonging to a proper Football League. The following week I received a number of phone calls and was told that we now had seven teams in our league, although some were not very thrilled about the long travel for each team on a Saturday morning. They conceded that some of the teams were very flush as far as their bank accounts were concerned, others were not as well off, so it was agreed that the league would pay half the travel fees and the clubs would pay half. This arrangement was put in place for the first season of the 'new' league, and thereafter each club did their own once more. This was agreed upon and ratified at the next meeting of the League, and the Local TV was there to assist in the ratification.

By this time our daughter Janine had returned from a 12 month working holiday in England where she lived and worked in Wimbledon as a chef for an ex-Lord Mayor of London. She fitted in a tour of Europe and also visited Ireland. On returning home she lived for some time in Melbourne and continued playing basketball with various teams, as she had done since her school days. She was a very competent basketball player and reached top grade in Melbourne and surrounds, playing centre for the Melbourne University Club, which played in the top grade of basketball in the state. The final year at this club produced a Most Valuable Player award. She continued playing when she and her husband, Ian, moved to Hervey Bay, where she was most sought after and received payment of expenses for playing for Hervey Bay Hurricanes in the southern conference competition once they had moved to Rockhampton. During this period she was five months pregnant and still playing well! Janine and Ian now have two of the most delightful girls one could wish to meet. Keeley the eldest of the two is presently training to be a veterinarian whilst Regan is presently doing a health science degree.

After many years we decided to put the slide business on the market and to that end we put it on the market with Kim Carter Real Estate. Although we had to wait a while to finalise a sale, it was achieved, and we were on our way to the Gold Coast and a whole lot closer to our grandchildren. Kim was a great saleswoman as far as Real Estate was concerned as she marketed and sold the several properties for us and a considerable number as far as the area was concerned.

GOLD COAST

As Janine and family had moved to the Gold Coast for Ian's work as an epidemiologist, it seemed logical to move to the coast. It was much easier to watch two little girls growing up from close by, rather than travelling all the way from Hervey Bay. We bought a little house in the area known as Studio Village and I kept myself amused renovating the home with a new kitchen and dining area. Then a bit more was added in the form of a new tiled entry, and my passion for painting was satisfied by re-doing the whole house on the inside.

After living in this house for about a year we decided it was too small, so we looked at numerous homes in the near vicinity and the adjoining area of Pacific Pines. We had just decided we would look at one more, and, after walking through the front door we both knew that it was the home we were going to buy, and we did just that. We lived here for three and a half years. It was during this period that I had a few problems with my health and was diagnosed to be in the early stages of Parkinson's disease. My doctor from Hervey Bay days had moved to the Coast years earlier so we were able to continue our relationship, and he appeared to have a good knowledge of my condition and duly pointed me in the direction of Professor Peter Silburn, who was listed with the qualification of being in the top five in the world as a neurologist. Appointments to see him were hard to obtain. I then found out that he was an expert in performing an operation known as Deep Brain Stimulation, which I decided to have, and a vacancy in his systems enabled me to have the operation within a few days. After the operation I was able to continue with my normal routine as if nothing had occurred.

After a couple of years in Pacific Pines we realized that in the future we would need a home where someone else did the work and we just lived there. Subsequently, we decided that we would move to an Over 50's Lifestyle in the near vicinity which took our fancy, and we have now been residents here for almost eleven years. During our residency we got to be good mates with Bob and Sandra Halliwell.

It was a strange coincidence that during a function in the clubhouse I ordered two glasses of red wine which I proceeded to carry back to the table. With my Parkinson's shake I was about to embarrass myself and spill them when a lady jumped up and grabbed them and carried them to the table for me. For that gesture I was forever grateful. Her name was Sandra Halliwell. Her husband Bob was a great AFL follower which we discussed at great length. I also mentioned that I had been a Victorian police man. He told me that he had an older brother who was in charge of the police driving school and I asked if his name was Keith to which he agreed. What a coincidence.

We attend all home games for the Gold Coast Suns and also nearby games such as the ones at the Gabba. The village also has a social Golf Club, so once a month we get to play some of the better golf courses on the coast including Royal Pines, where the Australian PGA is played. In recent years, when I was playing golf once or twice a week, I was playing off a regular handicap of

15. At the village we have a full size bowling green where I play on a regular basis, plus there is Indoor Carpet Bowls, a Gymnasium, a Library, indoor and outdoor pools and innumerable groups hosting all sorts of activities. The Metricon Stadium where the Gold Coast Suns AFL team plays is only ten minutes away. Coming April 2021 we will have lived here for 11 years, and the way things are shaping we are happy to continue. It may work out to be a contest where I'm still adding a new paragraph for every year and am still annoying you. But it may go the other way. It seems it may turn out to be a no-brainer, but I doubt that will be the case as there weren't too many there in the first place.

Then there was FRED. He was our racehorse, with grave doubts about his title as such, when he was placed last in the last race of the day at a race day in Penshurst, Victoria. When the race was underway he was placed last at the first bend and, when re-appearing, he was so far behind the rest of the field that we had to get the binoculars to see if it was actually Fred. We thought maybe he had run backwards for the short period we could not see him. When he eventually returned to the yard his trainer said to say goodbye to Fred (and you will notice his title reducing) as he ascended to the great race-course in the sky.

Goodbye fred.